Published 2025

Printed in Australia by IngramSpark

Library of Congress Cataloging-in-Publication Data is available from the National Library of Australia

Printed book: ISBN 978-0-6452519-3-7

E-book: ISBN 978-0-6452519-4-4

Author: Mary of Nazareth, as channeled by XO

Title: Full of Grace: A Mother's Journey Through Love, Loss, and Light

Disclaimer: This book contains messages that were received through spiritual channeling by an anonymous individual. The words within are offered as a work of devotion, inspiration, and contemplation. They do not represent official doctrine of any religious institution, nor are they intended to replace personal faith, critical thinking, or discernment. Readers are encouraged to receive these messages with an open heart and use their own inner guidance when reflecting on the content. Whether taken as metaphor, mystical insight, or direct spiritual communication, this work is shared in the spirit of love, humility, and reverence for the sacred.

TABLE OF CONTENTS

Chapter 1: The First Yes   7

Surrendering to the unknown when you are called before you feel ready.

Chapter 2: The Weight of Wonder   11

The early days of motherhood—sacred, sleepless, and full of holy mystery.

Chapter 3: Hidden Years, Holy Work   15

Raising a child in quiet, away from the world's gaze, and finding meaning in the ordinary.

Chapter 4: The Space Between Letting Go and Holding On   19

How a mother learns to release, again and again, without losing herself.

Chapter 5: A Sword Shall Pierce   23

Facing sorrow without bitterness when life does not protect what you love most.

Chapter 6: When He Was Lost   27

Trusting through fear when you lose sight of the one you were entrusted to guard.

Chapter 7: When No One Sees the Mother   31

The invisible labor of love, and Heaven's tender recognition.

Chapter 8: The Wedding Feast and the Quiet Push   35

Knowing when to speak, when to step back, and how a mother's nudge can awaken purpose.

Chapter 9: At the Cross   37

Standing where no mother wants to stand—and remaining rooted in love.

Chapter 10: After the Silence   39

Grief, waiting, and the mystery of hope when everything seems lost.

Chapter 11: The Women Who Wait   41

Sisterhood, sorrow, and the quiet strength women lend one another in life's hardest seasons.

Chapter 12: The Rising Light   43

Redemption and the gentle healing that follows even the darkest nights.

Chapter 13: For the Mothers of the World   45

A final blessing and reminder that your unseen devotion echoes beyond time.

She dedicates this little book to every child —

Born and unborn, lost and found, wandering and held.

FULL OF GRACE

CHAPTER 1:
THE FIRST YES

Surrendering to the unknown when you are called before you feel ready.

There is a silence that follows the voice of an angel.

Not the silence of doubt, but of weight. The kind that settles over your spirit when you know your life will never be the same.

I was young—yes, too young by most standards. But faith doesn't wait for the perfect age, the perfect preparation. It comes when it comes. And when the angel came, so did the calling.

"Do not be afraid, Mary."

What strange comfort that was. Because of course I was afraid. Not of the angel, but of what he announced. Of what would be asked of me. Of what I could not control.

But I listened. I opened. And I said yes.

Not because I understood.

Because I trusted.

That yes did not come easily. It was not without trembling. But it was real. It came from a place beyond certainty—a place called surrender.

That is where all true mothering begins.

In the yes that costs you your plan, your timing, your safety. In the yes that breaks something open in you before anything has yet begun.

I didn't know then what that yes would mean.

I didn't know it would carry me to Bethlehem, to Egypt, to Jerusalem, to the foot of a cross. I didn't know it would demand everything and give me even more in return.

But I know now.

And I would say yes again.

If you have been called—into motherhood, into purpose, into something far beyond your understanding—know this: you do not have to be ready. You only have to be willing.

God does not look for perfect vessels.

He looks for open ones.

And your yes—small as it may feel—is holy ground.

FULL OF GRACE

CHAPTER 2:
THE WEIGHT OF WONDER

The early days of motherhood—sacred, sleepless, and full of holy mystery.

FULL OF GRACE

The night He was born, the world did not pause. The stars did not stop turning. The inns were full. The streets dusty. Life went on, unaware.

But I had stopped.

Everything in me had stilled with wonder.

He came quietly—no trumpet, no thunder—just a rush of pain, a cry, and then the warmth of a newborn against my skin. My son. The Son. Fragile and small. His breathing fast, then calm.

He nursed. He slept. He stirred in dreams. And I watched.

What do you do when you hold heaven in your arms?

You swaddle it. You rock it. You kiss its forehead and hum lullabies into its hair. You change linens, soothe cries, and wonder at the weight of what you've been given.

Motherhood is not only a miracle. It is a mystery. A holy one.

No one tells you that the sacred feels so ordinary. That divinity arrives with spit-up and sore arms, with sleepless nights and endless feeding.

But perhaps that is where God always chooses to dwell—in the ordinary, the overlooked, the deeply human.

A MOTHER'S JOURNEY

I did not always feel holy in those days. I felt tired. I felt unsure. I felt the ache of learning how to be mother to a child who was both mine and not mine.

And yet, those days were woven with glory.

When Joseph held Him and whispered prayers. When shepherds arrived, breathless and amazed. When strangers bowed and kings offered gifts. When I laid Him down and touched His cheek and felt the weight of both wonder and responsibility.

These are the sacred days no one sees.

If you are in them—elbows-deep in diapers, in dishes, in doubts—please hear this: the holiness is here, too. Not in your perfection, but in your presence. Not in your strength, but in your surrender.

You do not have to feel radiant to be radiant.

You are carrying light.

Even now. Especially now.

FULL OF GRACE

CHAPTER 3:
HIDDEN YEARS, HOLY WORK

Raising a child in quiet, away from the world's gaze, and finding meaning in the ordinary.

FULL OF GRACE

There are entire years that Scripture does not mention—years where He grew, and I mothered, and no one wrote it down.

Those were not wasted years.

They were hidden, yes. But they were full.

Full of scraped knees and growing limbs. Full of bread rising in the morning and oil running low at night. Full of whispered prayers and quiet songs. Full of learning—His and mine.

No crowds. No miracles. Just life.

Sometimes, the most holy work is the most unseen. The daily tending. The patient forming. The love that repeats itself in small acts: folding linen, stirring pots, listening to stories, correcting gently, holding long.

He learned to walk in my kitchen. He learned to speak by watching me. I taught Him to knead dough, to sing psalms, to share, to forgive. I didn't always know what I was doing. But I knew how to love.

And love is enough.

In those years, I often wondered: Is this how salvation comes? Slowly? Quietly? Hidden in the dust of everyday life?

Yes.

Redemption does not always roar. Sometimes it is raised in secret, in small homes, by faithful hands.

If you are in the hidden years—raising children, building love, serving without applause—please know this:

He sees you.

God sees the ordinary and calls it sacred. He sees the tired eyes and the soft humming and the floors swept again and again. He sees the way you hold the world together with nothing but grace and grit.

These years matter.

They will not all be written down, but they are being recorded in heaven.

You are raising something holy.

Even when no one sees.

FULL OF GRACE

CHAPTER 4:
THE SPACE BETWEEN LETTING GO AND HOLDING ON

How a mother learns to release, again and again, without losing herself.

He grew.

He began to stretch beyond me—into the world, into Himself, into the mystery of who He was becoming. I saw it in the way He asked questions that unsettled even the elders. In the way He would look far off, as though seeing something I could not.

And my hands, once always holding, had to learn to open.

Letting go doesn't happen once. It happens in small moments: when they take their first steps away from you, when they speak words you didn't teach them, when they begin to carry a purpose greater than your plans.

It's one of the deepest griefs of motherhood—that to love them rightly, you must learn to release them.

And yet, there is a kind of holding that doesn't suffocate. A holding that says: I am still here. I will always be here, even when you go where I cannot follow.

That's the holy tension: to hold with open hands.

I did not always get it right. I worried. I asked too many questions. I followed too far, then stepped back too suddenly. But I was learning. As He grew in wisdom and stature, I was growing too.

A MOTHER'S JOURNEY

And I had to trust that what had been planted in silence and nurtured in ordinary years would rise strong when the time came.

If you are in that space—in the ache between holding on and letting go—know this: it is sacred ground.

To love someone deeply is to let them change, let them choose, let them go, and yet never let go of love itself.

You will always be mother. You will always carry their beginning. But you were never meant to be their end.

And when you release them into the world, you release them into the hands of the One who gave them to you in the first place.

That is trust.

That is love.

FULL OF GRACE

A MOTHER'S JOURNEY

CHAPTER 5:
A SWORD SHALL PIERCE

Facing sorrow without bitterness when life does not protect what you love most.

I remember the words spoken over me in the temple, when He was just a baby in my arms:

"A sword will pierce your own soul also."

At the time, I held those words quietly, unsure what they meant.

But over the years, I began to understand. Motherhood is pierced by pain.

Not always all at once. Sometimes slowly, in slivers. In seeing your child misunderstood. In knowing they are hurting and being unable to take it away. In watching them walk a path that will cost them everything.

I would have traded places with Him.

But that was not the story. This was not a path I could walk for Him. I could only walk beside Him—for as long as He let me. And then… beyond that, I could only watch.

The sword did not destroy me. But it cut deep.

There is a pain that is clean and there is a pain that lingers. This was both. And yet—I did not turn bitter. I could not. Because love remained.

I would not let grief take what love had built.

A MOTHER'S JOURNEY

If you are carrying a pierced heart—if you have watched someone you love walk through sorrow, illness, injustice, or loss—know this: you are not alone. There is a way through that does not require hardening. There is a way to grieve and still stay soft.

Your heart may break, but it can also widen. To hold more. To feel deeper. To become more tender, not less.

The sword may pierce, but love remains.

And sometimes, the deepest love is the kind that endures even when it cannot rescue.

FULL OF GRACE

CHAPTER 6:
WHEN HE WAS LOST

*Trusting through fear when you lose sight of
the one you were entrusted to guard.*

FULL OF GRACE

He was twelve.

We had traveled to Jerusalem, as we did every year. The city was alive with the festival—songs, spices, the sound of sandals on stone.

We prayed, we worshipped, we walked with thousands.

And then… we left.

We assumed He was with others in the caravan. With cousins or friends. But a day passed, and He was nowhere.

The panic came fast and hot.

I have never run like that. Never prayed like that. Not before, not since.

For three days, we searched. Through crowds, through alleyways, through shadows. Every mother's nightmare was suddenly my own.

How could I have lost the Son of God?

But in truth, I had not lost Him. He had chosen to stay behind—drawn to His Father's house, to the questions of elders, to the stirrings of His purpose.

We found Him in the temple, calm and speaking with authority far beyond His age.

"Why were you looking for Me? Did you not know I must be in My Father's house?"

And just like that, I realized: I would never fully grasp the path He was on.

He came home with us. He was still my child. But the letting go had begun.

If you've ever lost sight of the one you love—physically, emotionally, spiritually—if you've ever felt the terror of that absence, I know that fear. I know the breathlessness, the desperation, the doubt.

But I also know the moment when you find them again.

And even if they are not as they were—even if they have changed, grown, pulled away—they are still yours to love. Even if you no longer understand, you can still remain near.

You will not always hold them in your arms. But you will always hold them in your heart.

And no matter how far they seem from you, they are never far from God.

FULL OF GRACE

CHAPTER 7: WHEN NO ONE SEES THE MOTHER

The invisible labor of love, and Heaven's tender recognition.

I was there through it all.

Not always at His side, but always behind the scenes—watching, praying, tending. Not because I needed recognition, but because I loved.

Most people saw the crowds, the miracles, the teachings. They did not see the mother who raised the hands that healed the blind. The one who taught Him to walk, to listen, to care.

They saw the ministry. I saw the man.

And yet—how often did they forget me? Or overlook me entirely?

But God never did.

Heaven sees the unseen.

He sees the midnight feedings, the whispered prayers, the quiet endurance. He sees the sacrifices no one thanks you for. The love you give when you have nothing left. The way you keep showing up.

That is sacred work.

Not because it is noticed, but because it is true.

If you feel invisible—if your motherhood has been quiet, hidden, or uncelebrated—know this: what is hidden on earth is honored in heaven.

Your labor is not in vain. Your love is not unnoticed.

Even when no one sees the mother, God sees.

And He delights in every act of love, however small, however silent.

FULL OF GRACE

CHAPTER 8:
THE WEDDING FEAST AND THE QUIET PUSH

Knowing when to speak, when to step back, and how a mother's nudge can awaken purpose.

It was a celebration. A wedding. There was joy, and laughter, and wine—until the wine ran out.

It seemed like a small crisis to others. But I knew this was the moment.

I told Him, simply: "They have no more wine."

He looked at me—not with rejection, but with knowing.

"My hour has not yet come."

Still, I turned to the servants. "Do whatever He tells you."

It was not a demand. It was a release. A nudge.

The quiet push of a mother who knows when the time is right.

He turned the water into wine. The first miracle. The beginning.

Sometimes the most powerful thing a mother can do is step aside—yet speak the words that make space for the divine.

If you are at the edge of your child's unfolding—watching them step into something sacred—remember: your faith still matters.

Your voice, even whispered, still echoes.

You don't have to lead the way. You only have to believe in the light within them.

Sometimes, the quietest push is the holiest.

CHAPTER 9: AT THE CROSS

*Standing where no mother wants to stand—
and remaining rooted in love.*

There are places no mother ever wants to go.

The foot of a cross is one of them.

And yet, I stood there—because I could not leave Him. Not in His suffering. Not in His final hour.

I had once cradled Him as a newborn. Now I watched as the world crucified Him. The same hands that healed were pierced. The same voice that calmed storms cried out in pain.

And I stood.

Not because I was strong—but because I loved.

He saw me there. And even in agony, He made sure I was not alone.

"Woman, behold your son."

"Behold your mother."

In His final breath, He gave me to another. And gave me peace.

If you have ever stood at the edge of sorrow, helpless to change it—if you have loved through pain, remained in loss, and stayed rooted in what could not be saved—know this:

You have touched holy ground.

There is no deeper love than to remain in the face of suffering. Not to fix it. Not to flee it. But to stay.

And that is enough.

Love that stands at the cross is the kind that changes the world.

A MOTHER'S JOURNEY

CHAPTER 10:
AFTER THE SILENCE

Grief, waiting, and the mystery of hope when everything seems lost.

After the cross, there was silence.

A silence so complete it filled the air like smoke. We wrapped His body, placed it in the tomb, and rolled the stone shut.

And then we waited.

Sabbath passed. Long. Heavy. Still.

There were no words. Only memory. Only aching.

But somewhere in that stillness, hope stirred. Not loud. Just a whisper.

And then: He is risen.

I could hardly believe it. And yet—I knew it was true.

Grief had been real. Death had been real. But love… love was more real still.

If you are waiting in the silence—between loss and life, between despair and dawn—trust this: resurrection is real.

The light will come.

A MOTHER'S JOURNEY

CHAPTER 11:
THE WOMEN WHO WAIT

Sisterhood, sorrow, and the quiet strength women lend one another in life's hardest seasons.

In those days of grief and waiting, I was not alone.

There were women—faithful, fierce, and tender. They stayed. They waited. They wept beside me.

We carried spices. We kept watch. We remembered.

And when the resurrection came, it came to us first.

Not to the powerful. Not to the loud. But to the women who waited.

If you are waiting in sorrow, look around. You are surrounded. We wait together. And when light returns, we rise together.

This is sisterhood. This is strength.

CHAPTER 12:
THE RISING LIGHT

Redemption and the gentle healing that follows even the darkest nights.

The resurrection did not erase the wounds. His hands still bore them.

But He was alive.

And everything began to glow differently.

The ache remained, but it no longer ruled me. The grief softened.

The love remained. And joy returned—not loud, but deep.

Healing is slow. But it comes.

And when it does, let it come. Let it rise in you like dawn. Let yourself begin again.

Even after death, there is life.

Even after night, light returns.

CHAPTER 13:
FOR THE MOTHERS OF THE WORLD

A final blessing and reminder that your unseen devotion echoes beyond time.

FULL OF GRACE

To the mothers—seen and unseen, celebrated and silent—

You are holy.

Your love, your labor, your long nights and deeper prayers—they matter.

Heaven sees what the world overlooks.

You are part of a lineage of grace, of perseverance, of fierce and tender strength. You carry eternity in your arms, your hands, your heart.

You may feel weary. But you are radiant.

You may feel invisible. But you are remembered.

You may feel broken. But you are beloved.

I bless you—not as one above you, but as one among you.

You are not alone.

And your love—given in ordinary moments and quiet devotion—will echo long beyond your days.

Full of grace.

Full of light.

Forever a mother.

A MOTHER'S JOURNEY

ABOUT THE VOICE BEHIND THE BOOK

Full of Grace is a channeled transmission of love, wisdom, and remembrance—received in deep stillness by an anonymous soul devoted to listening. These words are not offered as doctrine, but as devotion: a quiet unfolding of Mary's presence as guide, mother, and mirror for all who walk the path of love. The writer remains unnamed, so that the voice of Mary may be felt more clearly—heart to heart, spirit to spirit.

xo

www.ingramcontent.com/pod-product-compliance
Lightning Source LLC
Chambersburg PA
CBHW032019290426
44109CB00013B/714